Praise for Michael McClure and

"Living poems, inhabited by living things! C
Our ancestors' blood running inside us. .
consciousness nesting where she can, to attract our cruel ga
have to do is kneel and look."   FRANCESCO CLEMENTE

"A dance of deep wit proceeds from a backbone of symmetry—McClure's trans-human view is grounded in proteins and ergs. This poetry is soulful freedom at play in the Desire-realm—echoing ballad, blues, old lyrics, as it turns and displays. Celebratory, elusive, freshly deliberate rituals—amazing."   GARY SNYDER

"Once again Michael McClure has brought us some beautiful poetry back from those shapely and scary pathways where spirit and biology have their torrid commingling. It's part of the poesy D.H. Lawrence once brought to such brilliance, a tradition McClure keeps very alive at the end of this smoky and blood-drenched century."   ED SANDERS

"Michael McClure is one of the few poets in America who has always been his own voice, and that voice is like no other."

NORMAN MAILER

"In his alchemical scriptorium, which becomes the reader's mind, Michael McClure undergoes brilliant and difficult changes of form. Ecstatic birthings of star, flower, grub, tyger, black neurons, cherubs in trenches crystallize moment to moment all over these pages. There is pain with them as there is with all labors; the sharpness of resultant raised senses, though, is equally brilliant and lovely. There is in his poetry what Marianne Moore demands, and what many others misunderstand, the raw and the geniune—the willingness of unwearied senses to be what they perceive."   ANNE WALDMAN

Rebel Lions

ALSO BY MICHAEL McCLURE

REBEL LIONS

MICHAEL McCLURE

A New Directions Book

Copyright © 1984, 1985, 1986, 1987, 1988, 1989,
1990, 1991 by Michael McClure

All rights reserved. Except for brief passages quoted in a newspaper, maga-
zine, radio, or television review, no part of this book may be reproduced in any
form or by any means, electronic or mechanical, including photocopying and
recording, or by any information storage and retrieval system, without
permission in writing from the Publisher.

ACKNOWLEDGMENTS

Grateful acknowledgement is given to the editors and publishers of books,
magazines, and broadsides in which some of the material in this volume
previously appeared: *Another Chicago Magazine, Arif Press, Artweek, Blue Mesa,
Book for Sensei, Caliban, Conjunctions, cold-drill, Cover, Exquisite Corpse,
Floating Island, Gas, Grand Street, Jay De Feo: Works on Paper, New Directions
in Prose & Poetry, New York Quarterly, Noh Quarterly, Pearl, Poetry Flash, San
Francisco Calendar, Table-Talk Press, The Threepenny Review, Venue, Zyzzyva.*

The quote from Rainer Maria Rilke's "Eighth Elegy" is from the Robert
Hunter translation of *Duino Elegies*, Hulogos'i Press (Copyright © 1987 by
Robert Hunter). The author expresses his thanks to Robert Hunter and to the
press.

The lines of Roque Dalton are from *Poemas Clandestinos*, Solidarity
Publications (Copyright © 1984 by Roque Dalton). The author expresses his
thanks to Solidarity Publications and to the translator, Jack Hirschman.

The line from Diane di Prima is found in "Rant," *Pieces of a Song,* City
Lights (Copyright © 1990 by Diane di Prima). The author expresses his thanks
to the poet and to City Lights.

Designed by Amy Evans
Manufactured in the United States of America
New Directions Books are published on acid-free paper.
First published as New Directions Paperbook 712 in 1991
Published simultaneously in Canada by Penguin Books Canada Limited

LIBRARY OF CONGESS CATALOGING-IN-PUBLICATION DATA
McClure, Michael.
    Rebel lions / Michael McClure.
       p.   cm.
    ISBN 0–8112–1164–9 (alk. paper)
    I. Title.
PS3563.A262R4   1991
811'.54—dc20   90–48705
                                                          CIP

CENTRAL ARKANSAS LIBRARY SYSTEM
LITTLE ROCK PUBLIC LIBRARY
700 LOUISIANA STREET
LITTLE ROCK. ARKANSAS 72201

CONTENTS

AUTHOR'S NOTE

Poetry is a muscular principle and it comes from the body—it is the action of the senses, of what is heard, seen, tasted, touched, and smelled as well as what is imagined and reasoned—it is the voice's athletic action on the page and in the world. Poetry is one of the edges of consciousness. And consciousness is a real thing like the hoof of a deer or the smell of a bush of blackberries at the roadside in the sun.

By 1955 I began centering poems so that it would be clear that they are the stuff of consciousness. The impulse to center the poems gave the writing a visual notation for the breath and voice as well as the reading mind, and it gave the poems the lengthwise symmetry found in higher animals. The centering also allowed the poems to have a body language on the page, and with the voice when spoken aloud. There were other reasons too, I could look at the integrity of the poems—as if they were creatures and be moved by their shapes. I was not interested in what was then called "form" but in the extension of content into a shape with an immediate relation to me and to the reader.

I was interested in the poem being alive in the air as well as on the page. The poem on the page troubled me because it seemed like such a thing of beauty, I wanted to remind the reader that it was, in fact, an object, and a seductive object because it was so close to being alive. By putting lines of capital letters in the text of the poem there was a disruption of the allure of the poem and a reminder that it was a made thing. The capitals worked on the one hand to distance the reader for a moment and, on the other, to create an attractive disruption of an otherwise flowing experience. Later I experimented with using the lines of capitals to signify a small shift of intensity in the voice or mind. The lines of capitals at the opening of the poem came to signify the quality of energy with which a poem begins. The capitals never mean that the lines are shouted or that they are chanted.

My poetry is mental poetry and it does not distinguish between mental and physical—it captures the movement of thought from perception to perception and leaves it flourishing in the normal animal energy that is our substance. I have been able to write with a language that feels like my own, and I have been able to absorb the ideas of spiritual autobiography and gesture from the art of painting. In an early book, *The New Book/A Book of Torture,* the careless accidents of typography, grammar, and spelling were left, as a painter might have left the energetic drips upon a canvas. The method that I have developed has allowed me to try to create poems that might become living things, and even the failure of that attempt has had an alchemical value for me. I have been able to write spontaneous booklength poems of autobiography and of biological and social consciousness such as *Rare Angel* and *Dark Brown* and my unpublished *Fleas.* This poetry has been initiated, in part, in the action plays that I wrote for theater in the '50s and '60s, *The Mammals,* and also in stage pieces of later decades such as *Josephine: The Mouse Singer.*

A trail moves through these various manners of experiment to *Rebel Lions.* The poem "Stanzas from Maui" is the central poem; though it reads well aloud, it is not a poem for performance, but in fact, a reification of an agonizing and joyful and sudden state of consciousness. Some poems in this volume are spontaneous and some are carefully and lengthily worked. "Stanzas from Maui" was honed for a long time. It reifies with voice and body energy, using repetition as the nervous system uses repetition, the exact moment in which one who is dying of one love falls in love again. Mallarmé said, "Poetry is the language of a state of crisis." He is correct, and "Stanzas from Maui" makes a verbal sculpture in the language of a state of crisis. It can be seen that this poem's manner springs from what I have already done in other poems.

I am continuing to give readings of my poetry at colleges and theaters; for the past several years I have also worked with The Doors keyboardist Ray Manzarek. Ray plays piano while I read the poems. Some of the poems in this book were written with this artistic symbiosis in mind: "High Heels," "Foreman and Ali," and "Czechoslovakia" are examples. These have joined a repertoire that includes biological and political and environmental poems from *Antechamber & Other Poems,* and from *Fragments of Perseus* and *Jaguar Skies.*

When I picture lions I think of the lions I saw in Kenya and Tanzania on my first trip to East Africa in 1973. Some large mammals have a special state of consciousness which is at once curious and calm and yet passionately involved in the physical facts of life and the world.

A rebel lion is a spirit in revolt against his or her own custom and habit. The title celebrates not only my own breakthrough ("Rise, like lions after slumber," said Shelley) but is a thank-you to all of our predecessors in art and science who are, and have been, rebel lions.

Michael McClure

Rebel Lions goes out with a huge load of *gracias* from the author to many friends and dear ones. The first ones that come to mind are Amy Evans, my family—especially daughter Jane McClure—Harry Hunt, Robert Duncan, Bruce and Jean Conner, Norma Schlesinger, Judith Hunt, Charles Olson, Jim Morrison, Hans and Pam Peeters, Richard Felger, Allen Ginsberg, Wesley Tanner, J. Laughlin, Gary Snyder, Sterling and Diane Bunnell, Jules Weiss, the instructors and administration of the California College of Arts and Crafts—and, for his input into this book, editor Peter Glassgold.

M.M.

*Mi poesía
es como la siempreviva
paga su precio
a la existencia
en término de asperidad.*

My poetry's
like the everlasting
paying for its price
to life
in rough-edged terms.

ROQUE DALTON

THE ONLY WAR THAT MATTERS IS THE WAR
AGAINST THE IMAGINATION

DIANE DI PRIMA

OLD
FLAMES

FOR LOVE

SEE THE MORNING'S RED AND BLACK AND BLUE
AND WHITE AND YELLOW!
First there is the roar and then the silence
then the beat of hammers on new boards
then the hollow dragging of a crowbar over concrete.
These cannot disperse the memory of the striding
of a jaguar, stepping, turning, twisting,
with muscles moving under thumbprint spots
on orange fur—or the white-mustached
marmosets that hug each other
with their love-made arms
and spidery and minuscule
fingers. CAN THEY
make trails through Time?

CAN WE? Do they soul-make
like a datura blossom withering
in the morning feeding flies?

I'LL

STAND

AND

BE ME,

this spirit that I am!

That's supernatural!

─────────────

No more is needed but the scent of lavender
and burning feathers.

I am much more than doglike bones
and the changing of the weather!

Pulsebeat of rubies. Breath of precious stones.

White howls of wolves and moss's moans!

The seen and unseen are swirling
in the gloaming

while we dress up to go aroaming
so late into the night!

I love your footstep with delight!

BONFIRE IN THE SNOWS

I'LL CLAIM THE CATERPILLAR
IN THE ROSE!!

I LOVE HIS EYES AND INSECT TOES!

He has black spots that see and purple sides;
his mouthparts chew through the day and night.
He matches one inside of me
who's stretched out languorously and gnawing.
Rose petals change to lion's face upon his wings.
When he comes out then I go within!
You'll know me
by the grains of pollen on my chin.

There's an eye upon each wing!

When he flaps there's flare of lightning!

I am Rose and Grub

and

growing!

I can sing within the howling
making music in the summer air.

———————

BREAST!

SMILE!

Desire unleashed.

Cherubs tortured in the trenches.

Dark wine splattered on the fences.

Smiles of moment burst from torment.

Like a bug within the rose
I'll be the thing I am

and I'm the bonfire in the snows.

THE SILKEN STITCHING

"Écrasez l'infâme!"
SMASH THE SYSTEM!

AND DAMN THE SYSTEM CRUSHING US
GODDAMN THE FEAR THAT HALTS
our Art and Love and twists into the robot shapes
that spray out baths of lies
and drizzle sewage in
the spirit's ears and eyes.
The taste of bread and honey is gone
into an iron maw
and the kiss upon the breast has been spent
to
buy
a plastic claw!

Within the fearful glory of our dreams
a chubby angel is picking at
the silken stitching
of the seams!
AND
he

will laugh and fly,
AND HE WILL FLY
on
turquoise wings!

His bombs are worse than those we build.

His hands are in the gloves.

He's the wind that's whirling clouds
of feathered wolves and vengeful doves!

AWAKENING AND RECALLING A SUMMER HIKE

bird shadows in the room

WINGED SHADOWS PRESSING FEATHERS
ON THE WALL
recall the intellect of site and place
THAT
MAKE
this burst of Soul
from lichened granite boulder
where the coyote passes perky as a jackal,
smiling to himself
—and I breathe deep
to see the swooping golden eagle
sensing me inside the brake
of oak and sycamore and maple
where farewell-to-springs are blooming
in the dawn of summer.
My arm grows whole among
white-rippled chert
and minty smell of sage.
THE RAGE
to be
and complicate and fly,
is smoldering as
the delicacy of a baby's dreams
and the clear genius of a stroke of thunder!

KEATS,

you

are

RIGHT,

the intellect of place is true delight!

There goes the whippoorwill who charms the night!

TO AN INCHWORM

HEY THERE, LITTLE ONE, I TURN YOU LOOSE
after all this tickling
you make upon my hand—while you frantic-wave
your almost brainless head with huge gold-yellow eyes.
I like the pinstripe on your sides
and the madcap vivacity with which
you boogey, making strands
of many scaredy footprints.
You're a busy creature who knows that he's
tasty viands
for someone bigger
—maybe shiny wasp or the trigger
clasp of mantis.
Hey, there! Run loose
among the flowers and the sedum,
even yogis and zen masters
have no more freedom
than an open-end permission
to chew on petals and wriggle through
the nests of bronzy thorns!
You and I are just the same
—we once were "borns!"

THE MURDERS IN
CALAVERAS COUNTY

WHAT IS THE SCENT OF BABY'S BREATH AND
MANGLED BONE THAT'S INTERMIXED WITH MURDER?
Who are these ogres in the foothill's dreams
that burn and powersaw and torture?
I know the mindless hate and I'm distraught and jarred.
The killings of the innocents, the stumbling boys and girls,
tears my sleep to senseless fields
and leaves me twisting in the dark
with mindless sickened wonder
like the times that we sent bombers
SCREAMING TO THE EAST,
AND I'M AGHAST.
The torments built will last
forever
in each moment's endlessness.
The stench of human cruelty creates a cloud
that does not pass.

We must kneel and look upon the moth
that's resting on the pane

and touch the yellow buttercup

and find the self that smiles again;

LET'S

FIND

what smiles again

and flounders in the neon-sewage net

and lift it out and breathe on it

and shield it from the rain.

———————

We can make new squadrons and new tents!
We're born with naught and grow the Heart's deep sense.

DARK BROWN EYES OF SEALS

THE CRUNCH OF GUILT WITHIN THE NECK
BITES THE MUSCLES OF THE JAW
at memory's site of what is beautiful
of sexuality and bliss.
(This takes the silent, active shapes
of secrets deep within—and then we do not know
what is *out* or *here* or *in*.)
THE
MEMORY
itself
is an infant's phantasm—locked in living-out
a strangling or a luscious kiss
that swirls in dripping chocolate
and gentle hurricanes
of milky arms and breasts.
The unknown pseudopods entwine
to make our spirits into streaming jewels
just as each higher cell
has become a pulsing pirate chest
wherein we are sleeping wolves
and singing angel fools

and
all
this
coils

and intercoils

and we stand on tiptoe
to bend and see our heels.

The air we breathe with deepening breath
is alive with birth and death.

We're held by the living arms of gods,
and moving through the summer waves
we're watched
by dark brown eyes of seals.

THE BULKS OF HEART

DEEP AND DEEPER GOES THE SEARCH
then spreads with sharklike fin
above the whitecap of the moment
where the bulks of things are in a foment,
blossoming in life. Imagination dives
again—myriadness agape—
sniffing shape after shape:

A BLUE-BLACK PLUM

A STARRY CANDLE IN THE DARKNESS

SOUND OF HAMMER ON A WOODEN DRUM

SKULL OF DEER

THE TOUCH OF THUMB
upon forefinger

THEN

THE WONDROUSNESS

BENEATH

IT

all!

The child is there!
Not in a snare
but
singing.

Tulips shadowing a hare
that's sleeping.

Sun beating yellow fields of wheat
and reapers' shadows reaping
while the women cook up pies and stews.

A boy's dream of the yew
that Robin used
to make his Greenwood bow

AND
ALL
THOSE
GALAXIES
OUT THERE

from which I stride!!!!!

No place for the Heart to hide!

ROSE
RAIN

STANZAS FROM MAUI

WE ARE DEEP INSIDE

WE ARE DEEP INSIDE

WE ARE DEEP INSIDE
WE ARE DEEP INSIDE
WE ARE DEEP INSIDE
WE ARE DEEP INSIDE
WE ARE DEEP INSIDE
WE ARE DEEP INSIDE
WE ARE DEEP INSIDE
WE ARE DEEP INSIDE, DEEP INSIDE IN CAVES,
in caves of caves, and precipices' mountain caves
like caves in the mountains out there,
in the mountains out there, where fog pours over cliff
ravines on green hillsides, where fog pours over cliff
ravines, as the air pours over the glass transom
in this room on Maui

WHERE ENTERING INTO THIS DEAR ONE,
IN THIS LOVE,
inside this one
I feel the earth
I feel the earth
I feel the earth in torment
that I have put out there
I have put it out there
I feel it here inside of me
inside of us
IN THIS BED
in this warmth, it is here

IT OVERWHELMS ME

OVERWHELMS ME
OVERWHELMS ME

MEATS ME   MEATS ME
IT   MEATS   ME, MEATS ME

MEATS ME, SUCKS ME IN, SUCKS ME IN

I'M GOING IN, MY GOD, I'M HERE
I'M GOING IN,
MY GOD, I'M HERE
I'M GOING IN, MY GOD, I'M HERE

and
A
N
O
T
H
E
R

THIS OTHER

SAVES
me!
This one saves me.
SHE'S HERE.
SHE'S SAVING ME.
I'm saved.
THANK YOU KWANNON,
THANK YOU KWANNON,
THANK YOU GODDESS
THANK YOU BODHISATTVA
OF COMPASSION
THANK YOU KWANNON

MY GOD, IT'S HUGE IN HERE,
THERE,
HERE,
MY GOD, IT'S HUGE IN HERE / THERE /
here, my god, my goddess,
my god, my goddess, thank you, Kwannon

THANK YOU, PYTHON PAPA

THANK YOU, PYTHON PAPA

We're meating, we're meating! It's black raw meat,
it's black raw meat in here,
it's black raw meat we're meating
Thank you, Kwannon. Thank you, Python Papa
Thank you for your mercy
Thank you for your strength
Thank you for your power
Thank you for your justice

It's black raw meat we're meating,
we're meating in these caves,
WE'RE MEATING IN THIS CAVE
WE'RE MEATING IN THIS CAVE

IS THIS? / THIS *IS* / FEAR AND
OH
MY,
NO,
GOD,
NOT
YES
IT IS,
OH
CHRIST
INSIDE OF HER

INSIDE OF HER
INSIDE OF HER
INSIDE OF YOU
HER
HERE
YOU
HER
MY LOVER
MY LOVER
HERE.

I'M WEEPING
I'M WEEPING WHERE
I'm weeping where that
other hurt me,
other hurt me, other hurt me,
INTERMINABLY, INTERMINABLY, INTERMINABLY.
You hurt me interminably
as I hurt you
A
S
your
Father Hurt You
as my Mother Hurt Me

I BLAME YOU
I BLAME YOU
I BLAME YOU
I BLAME YOU
I BLAME YOU
I BLAME YOU
I BLAME YOU
I BLAME YOU FOR THIS
I BLAME YOU FOR THIS
I BLAME YOU FOR THIS

I FORGIVE YOU
I FORGIVE YOU
I SEE IT IS
THE CLIFF OF MEAT-BLACK
IT IS THE CLIFF OF MEAT-BLACK
IT IS THE CLIFF OF MEAT-BLACK
it is the black cliff of meat back there. Yeah,
I'm crying
that's me crying
Hear me crying
Yeah, that's me, I'm crying,
I'm crying out

AND THIS DEAR FRIEND
THIS DEAR FRIEND
my dear friend
THIS DEAR FRIEND
this dear friend holds me
HUGS ME
SPEAKS TO ME

she holds me, hugs me, speaks to me
IN THIS CAVE
IN THIS CAVE OF BLACKNESS

I MEAN TO TELL YOU WHO ARE LISTENING
hearing of this meating
THAT
I'M
THAT WE'RE,
MATING
mating, that we're mating,
THAT WE'RE MATING, THAT WE'RE MATING,
THAT WE'RE MEETING AND WE'RE MATING
AND I FORGIVE ALL OTHERS
in this act

this art
this fact
this coupling
this fantasy
this imagining of nature.

I MEAN TO TELL YOU
WHO ARE LISTENING
that we're mating,
meeting,
mating,
and I forgive all others in this art
this act
this fact
this coupling
this fantasy
this imagining of nature.

AND I SAY, IT'S SO DEEP YOU'LL NEVER KNOW
IT'S SO DEEP YOU'LL NEVER KNOW
IT'S SO DEEP YOU'LL NEVER KNOW
IT'S SO DEEP YOU'LL NEVER KNOW
IT'S SO DEEP YOU'LL NEVER KNOW
IT'S SO DEEP YOU'LL NEVER KNOW
IT'S SO DEEP YOU'LL NEVER KNOW
IT'S AS DEEP IN MEAT,
IT'S AS DEEP IN MEAT,
IT'S AS DEEP IN MEAT—IT'S VERY DEEP—
it's as deep in meat as you are
sitting, standing, reading
glancing at this stream, this screen,
this repetition of the flash of speaking.
YOU'RE IN THERE
YOU'RE IN THERE
WE'RE FREE
I'M FREE

YOU'RE IN THERE
you're free, I'm free, you're in there,
we're free, I'm free, you're in there.
It's so deep, so deep you'll never know.
It's as deep as you are
It's as deep as you are
We're as deep as you are
It's as deep as it is
WE'RE AS DEEP AS YOU ARE IN THE CAVES
WHERE THE FOG FLESH MOVES IN FLOWING CLOUDS
IT'S AS DEEP AS YOU ARE IN THE CAVES
WHERE THE FOG FLESH MOVES IN FLOWING CLOUDS.

HEAR THAT, HEAR THAT, HEAR THAT
I CAN STOP CRYING
I can stop crying
YOU HEAR THAT?
YOU HEAR THAT?
I can stop crying
YOU CALL THIS GRIEVING?
YOU CALL THIS GRIEVING?
THIS IS GRIEF
that's me
that's me
LOOK, LOOK, THIS IS GRIEF
hear that, hear that, hear that,
this is grief
hear that, hear that howling,
hear that crying
YOU CALL THAT GRIEVING?
This is grief, hear that!

This other body / face / pair of eyes
This other body / face / pair of eyes
loves me. This other body, other body,

face, pair of eyes loves me, loves me.
I'M INSIDE
I'M INSIDE
I'M DEEP INSIDE
this Cave of Wonder. I'm deep inside this
CAVE OF WONDER
and I'm erect here, erect here,
I'm erect here
NOW
BORN.
NEW
BORN.
NEW
BORN.
NOW BORN
NEW BORN
IN HERE
in arms and gut and deep
in arms and gut and deep
in arms and gut and deep-
er in than ever. IT'S O.K.
IT'S O.K.
IT'S FINE. It's fine
Is that me? Is that me screaming? Howling?
That me howling? Howling? Am I crying?
My God, My Christ, lover
YOU
CARE

YOU
HOLD
ME

YOU
CARE

YOU
HOLD
ME

YOU
CARE

YOU HOLD ME
I'
M
YOURS

I'
M
YOURS

YOU
CARE

YOU
HOLD
ME

I'M
YOURS

I'
M
YOU'RS

I'
M
YOURS

YOU
CARE

YOU
HOLD
ME

I'
M

Y
O
U
R
S

YES YOURS   YES YOURS   YES YOURS

BUT THAT'S NOT HALF OF IT
NO, THAT'S NOT HALF OF IT
NOT HALF OF IT
NOT HALF OF IT

WE'RE ONE BEING   WE'RE ONE BEING
WE'RE ONE BEING
WHEN WE DO THIS
WE'RE DOING THIS
WE'RE DOING THIS
THIS IS WHAT WE'RE DOING
WE'RE DOING THIS

THIS IS SPONTANEOUS AND PLANNED
SPONTANEOUS AND PLANNED
as the wave ruffle, wave ruffle, wave ruffle, ripple
ripple, payload, payload, payload
of tiny shells, tiny tiny shells in the surf lap
tiny tiny shells in the blue warm surf lap
when you pick up a handful
when you bend, plunge hands into the surf,

and pick up a handful
of tiny shells in the surf lap
pick up a handful of tiny shells and hold them to the sun
—all tiny shapes and colors—pink, mauve, brown, and foamy
—pink mauve white brown, blue flash, silver foaming,
and hold them to the sun
hold them to the sun
hold them to the sun
hold them to the sun
hold them to the sun
hold these shells upward to the sun
hold these shells upward to the sun
shells upward to the sun
shells upward to the sun
shells upward to the sun
hold these shells upward to the sun
outward in your hand
OUTWARD IN YOUR HAND
UPWARD IN YOUR HAND AND PALM
UPWARD IN YOUR HAND AND PALM

and I'll hold back and keep, and I'll
hold back and keep, contain (even on this island
EVEN ON THIS ISLAND
EVEN ON THIS ISLAND)
a piece, a particle / a piece, a particle / a chunk,
a grope, a grasp, a hunk of grief, a hunk of grief,
BE-
CAUSE,
BE-
CAUSE IT'S ME, it's me, it's me. IT'S ME.

DEEP INSIDE
YEAH
DEEP INSIDE
I'll keep a shade of it

I'll keep a shade of it
I don't renounce the shade I keep of it
I don't renounce it. I don't renounce it.
I don't renounce it. And I praise
my lover.
MY LOVER
MY LOVER
PRAISE MY LOVER
who with her body with her voice
with her body with her voice
calls to creatures
CALLS TO CREATURES
CALLS TO CREATURES
calls me
like a handsome, lunky / handsome lunky /
giant horse, like a giant horse, to her.
Calls me like a handsome, lunky
giant horse to her
LIKE A HORSE TO HER

Praise my lover
Praise my lover
Praise my lover
Praise Kwannon!
Praise Kwan Yin!
Praise Kwannon!
Praise the Goddess! Praise the Goddess!

Praise to Python Papa.
Thank you Python Papa.
Praise to Python Papa.

PRAISE

PRAISE

PRAISE TO PYTHON PAPA

IN THIS REAL IMAGINATION! IN THIS REAL
IMAGINATION! IN THIS REAL
IMAGINATION! PRAISE KWAN YIN
PRAISE TO PYTHON PAPA
REAL IMAGINATION
WE'RE IN // I'M IN

YOUR BODY, YOUR BODY, REAL IMAGINATION!

PRAISE MY LOVER
PRAISE MY LOVER
PRAISE MY LOVER

PRAISE KWANNON
PRAISE KWAN YIN
PRAISE TO KWANNON

PRAISE TO PYTHON PAPA
PRAISE PYTHON PAPA
PRAISE PYTHON PAPA

PRAISE MY LOVER
WE ARE DEEP INSIDE
PRAISE MY LOVER
WE ARE DEEP INSIDE
PRAISE MY LOVER
WE ARE DEEP INSIDE

PRAISE THE MORNING

PRAISE MY LOVER

PRAISE THE MORNING

PRAISE THE MORNING

PRAISE THE MORNING

PRAISE THE MORNING

PRAISE THE MORNING

YEAH

PRAISE THE MORNING

GOETHE'S WORDS

for Amy

AND I AM STILL LEARNING THE SHAPE
OF THE LOVELY BOSOM;
though they are small
and soft-nippled
they
are plump
with the milk
of
kindness.
Love,
like a scarlet
maple leaf,
is where
one finds
it
!

The sunset is black
and green and purple
and there's the smell of pine smoke.
We are the hurdles
that we leap
to be ourselves.

REBEL LIONS

THE STATEMENT OF THE ROARING SELF
—THE SCOPE—THE STATURE!!
YEAH! RATHER THAN THE MIRE OF RESPOND . . .
I WILL NOT GIVE IN TO LESS
than my own presence and the gorgeousness
of the violence in things that Gautama saw. I WILL

OUT-SPEAK THEM, SPEAK OUT REAL THINGS
ALIVE WITH BELIEF
in the Night-Sky-Organism overhead—
the huge, streaming being of star arms and organs
with a chorus of coyotes playing around it,
and by day an eagle over the pool.

THEN, HERE, WRITING WITH THIS TYPER,
THIS MACHINE, I FIND
I DO NOT CONTAIN A ROBOT
—I AM NOT ROBOTICIZED
(THOUGH I WAS FASCINATED BY THAT IMAGE)
I'M NOT ROBOTICIZED IN MY SEXUAL
impulses—though I was driven to grasp at all women—.

NO, I AM NOT DRIVEN OR ORDERED
BY STRUCTURAL SHIT

that has become an armature inside of me

DIRECTING MY GESTURES.

NO!

BUT THERE WAS AN EN-FLESHIFICATION
of the infant psyche, of the spirit, of the breath

of lust.
        Call it anything (Freudian, Jungian) but it's
        IN DEEP BEHAVIOR, down deep inside
AND IT'S ALL THE LUSTY AND LUSTFUL EXPLOSIONS
        of infancy and boyhood and manhood,
        all tenebrous and glowing,
        turning wisps of spirit into this *me*
        —and it is a real thing with strong meaning
        but it is not robot-metallic it
        is a streaming, a flowing like cytoplasm
        and the rush of galaxies spreading this
        pulsing of everything. And I am capable
of kindness and forgiving and asking a new friend
to come and lie on my bed. Come lie with me here

        IN THIS LIVING THING

WE MAY BE REBEL LIONS   AND SURELY WE ARE
        REBELLIONS IN THIS GREAT REBELLION.
                WE ARE IN WAR
                against nothingness though we stand

                        on it!

        ROARING OUR SWEET WAR

—sensing the tips of our fingers and souls going back
        in streams and flashes to the first beginning.
And these actions I take go back in double layers
        —first to the meat that is made for me,
        and second, to the flesh I make of that

        AND I AM PROUD

        YES PROUD

YES PROUD

PROUD AND NEWLY GLOWING

AND PROUD PROUD

PROUD

OF

it!

My chest heaves up and I breathe free as the night sky!

Take these solid thoughts.

Take these solid thoughts,
they're a wing on which you can fly.

This is unchained and free of the lie!

What is all this but colored dust on the wings of a butterfly?

AND IT IS HUGE AS OUR SOULS
and it is freed, yes freed, of all goals

and we are fools, otters, foxes, lions, kings, queens and foals
—fools, otters, foxes, lions, kings, queens and foals!

ROSE RAIN

RAIN ON THE ROSES,
BLUE SKY,

and
you

on my
mind.

Nothing could be kinder.

I'm finding

the way.

Let's play
each day

like mayflies
in December

like stars

in the eternal
sky!

THE CHALLENGER
MONUMENT

for Isamu Noguchi

O
IVORY
CINDER
OPEN PETALS
SOAR THE SPACE PATH
FLESH SPIRITS, HEROES

McAuliffe Onizuka Jarvis
McNair Smith Resnik Scobee

NAVAJO BRACELET

I'VE GOT A NAVAJO BRACELET THAT SHIMMERS
WHEN I SING.
I've got a Navajo bracelet that shimmers when I sing.
I've got hands all over you and I feel everything.

You put your sweet body in my face
and what I smell is skinny love and lace.

This airplane flight is coming straight and true.
The ropes have left my fingers black and blue.

The desert dust is in my hair.
My eyes have got that canyon stare.

—And I'm flying to the sunlight of your face.

COKE KICK!

THERE'S A DEMON ON THE RAZOR
SUCKING ON THE BLADE.
I meet him on the freeway and I hug him in the shade.
His white forktail is caught inside my nose
and my black and blue eyes twitch spastic toes
as I sliver up the tapdance hill,
and feel the crushing of imagination's glow
into the crudest things a man can know.

THERE'S A RING STRUCK THROUGH MY NOSE!

A cord is lying on the mirror's shine!

Put it through the ring and lead me round and down
while I believe I'm high.

I

SNUFFLE

when I breathe. Writhe me in
these clouds of shame. Again!

Again!
Again!

AND THEN I STOP.
I AM THE ANIMAL I KNOW I AM,
I flush away this powder with the shit,
and I rise—an eagle-winged assassin—
the murderer of custom and of habit.
I flush away
this funny powder with the shit,

I'm a breathing rose!,
an eagle-winged assassin,
(I'M A BREATHING ROSE!)
the murderer of custom and of habit.

I STAND FREE.

I STEP FREE.

THIS ME.

HIGH HEELS

YOU'RE THE HIGH-HEELED BITCH INSIDE
THE MOVIE!

I'M THE HAIRY BEAST WHO'S BRUSHING
AT YOUR KNEES!

MY YELLOW EYES ARE STARING!

YOU'VE GOT ME CRAZY JERKING ON THE LEASH!

Don't break my neck—I'll hate you! HEY,
don't slash the screen with screams.
See my paws upon your belly.
Feel my breath upon your skull.
We're the leaf that's spinning in the Autumn
of the fall.
Stuff my ears with snow to cease
the creaking of the rack
and the black cock crowing in the shadow of the axe.
I've got you.
YOU'VE GOT ME.

WHAT DOES IT MEAN
IF WE MELT TOGETHER
in a pool of rippling
silver?

I'VE GOT A SOUL I'M BUILDING.

I'M SOUL MAKING.

You're setting fire to my edges.

That smoke is Future-Me!

You're walking on my fingers
while you're kissing all my toes.

We're the lake between the bonfires
burning in the snow.

STOP THE REEL,
I'VE
SEEN
THE TRAILER!

I'VE SEEN THE PREVIEW OF THE MOVIE!

There are killers around the corner;
there are murderers right there
—one is *El Presidente,*
one's a duck and one's a lop-eared hare.

Grenades are sailing. We got explosions
in the air.
I'm a cinder. I'm a cinder of a soul.
I'm soul-making in the movie.
We got explosions in the air.

Someone's blowing pieces off of babies in the cradle.
We got helicopters / I know we're able.
Stop the engines! Shred the system!
This is fantasy not liberation.
We're all squirreled together in this configuration.

THEN BLACKNESS BLOWS THE CANDLE
LIKE THE LIPS OF SHIVA

and I'm nothing dancing

AND I'M NO THING DANCING

and I'm nothing dancing

NO THING DANCING

a coal-colored blot

IN THE BLACKNESS

OF A MINDLESS STARE . . .

a black thing of music in the midnight air.

STOP THE REAL I'VE SEEN THE PREVIEW

and I'm nothing dancing

nothing dancing

IN THE BLACKNESS

OF A MINDLESS STARE.

BLACK IVORY

I AM HERE AND I STRETCH THROUGH
THE SILVER CONSTELLATIONS
and hand you the carving
that I made in my other body;
it's a sinuous bear's head
of ivory turned black
by aeons of permafrost
AND

I

STARE
INTO

the glass;
your reflection
is next to mine.

WE ARE MADE OF THE SAME STUFF!

For what is spirit but another chunk
of Black Ivory?

Pre-Columbian Eskimo Carvings
Lowie Museum of Anthropology

BERKELEY SONG

POWER—GLORY—SCANDAL—MOVIES
—T.V.—SEX—
that is all the SOCIAL WHIRLING
that is the thrilling box that uses up
OUR HEADS
but I hug you in peyote-colored morning
where Master Mozart is singing doves
and robins back to sleep.
This touching of our hands and feet
is the velvet curtain that we keep
AS
WE
DIVE INTO THE DAY
TO FLARE LIKE STARS

making daily layers
interspersed with dreams.
WHERE THE GRIEF OF EVERY BEGGAR
hurts me in my seams.
I'm getting threadbare in my spirit.

WHAT DOES THIS MEAN?

I'll get myself an uzi and blast bursts at this machine.

WHY ARE ALL THESE PEOPLE STARVING?

Come back, Che Guevara, we didn't mean to kill you!
We were parading in the streets.
There was even tear gas and we weren't hiding
in the silken sheets.

I hug my lover in peyote-colored morning
where Master Mozart is singing doves
and robins back to sleep.

PRINCESS BRIDE

I WEEP FOR OUR LOVE PRINCESS,
FOR I AM ENCHANTED AND OLD
IN THE MOVIE
BUT
here in the real world
I AM THE JAGUAR
licking your sleek
HAUNCH
on the cliff edge
with the city below
in the silver fog
where
your
HUG
is good
for a trillion
years.
What is life
but a vale of fears
and a child's mask
on the muzzle
of a snake?

We stand knee-deep
in the lake
and side-by-side
in our waking sleep.

Capistrano Beach

POLITICS OF THE SOUL

IN THE MIND THE COMPARTMENTS OF
PAIN ARE RUTS!
The personality is wrinkled like a nut
and rippled with imagined griefs becoming real
but somewhere in the starving world
WE MUST STRETCH OUT AND FEEL
the panhandler dying by the brick wall
and scratch his black, greasy dog
on the head—otherwise we are dead
inside our music and satin rooms.
We're so busy healing ourselves!
WE'RE SO-O-O-O BUSY HEALING OURSELVES
but these compartments of pain
IN OUR HEADS
are rifts in satin,

WHILE

OUT

THERE,

while out there,

a revolution is dying to be born.

AND WE MUST FACE, YEAH, FACE THE POLITICS
of the soul
and feel the fur under our hand!

.

Fly with the eagle and burrow with the mole!

LEADBELLY BLUES

LEADBELLY BLUES GET IN MY BONES
I'm sick of old folks' tears and baby's groans.
I'm choke full of this lion-eating Rome.
I'm going where the eagle is going.
Zero, America, I'm going home.
I'll be where I hold my lover at night.
My head's a hammer and my toes are stones.
She's got a bed the color of a rose.
Rain on the roof in the morning light.
Leadbelly blues get in my bones.

Rain on the roof in the morning light.

WHITE BOOT

in Golden Gate Park after the storm

STERLING BELIEVES THAT CHAOS ARISES
FROM DEEP INTRINSIC ORDER
and is merely a quality of energy
in the scene that surrounds.
ORDER, he asserts, is earlier
than this universe,
and precedes what a finger
or tongue touches on now;
order enhances and shapes
the buttercup and the moss
stirring on the storm-soaked ground
as well as the shark-colored jay that flies
to take popcorn from my hand.
Even the junco
there by my white boot
on the dripping flagstones
knows it.
The hail intermingling in silvery stripes
with the downrush of rain,
is the same structure as thought.
The flesh of the resonating psyche is free
and cannot be bought.
—BUT
ALL
SOME
KNOW
of such things
is the nuggetlike gold of hunger,
the rippling muscle of ongoing love,
and the light that flashes
from a wild eye.

DISTURBED BY FREEDOM

MY HAND IS A GUN AND EACH FINGER
IS A BARREL
and my arm is growing stretching reaching
like a DREAM and I don't know
what to shoot, surely not the robins who have flown
ALL
the way
BACK
from the mountains of Sonora over the desert
where I have driven amazed at the craggy
strangeness of raw beauty.
((THAT'S WHAT I AM ABOUT: BEAUTY.
—BEAUTY AND SENSE))
and these robins have alighted here
in these green meadows where sprinkled water
turning warm runs over the masses of pink blooms.
I CANNOT SHOOT THE SOUND OF THE TRAFFIC.
A hundred bullets
would not stop that bus and I
would not hurt the children
or the adolescents at the moving windows
with their pink mohawk haircuts
and their sexual cries
LIKE HUMAN MACAWS.
It is another day and another dollar.
I
WONDER
WHERE
I
AM
((ROAMING SO SWEETLY FROM FIELD
TO FIELD DIS-
TURBED BY MY FREEDOM!))

—AND LOOK AT THE DEEP SCRATCHES THAT MADMEN
make with their keys on the sleek red
lacquer of my car.
I taste coffee in my mouth.
MY MOUTH IS WHERE I AM LIVING TODAY
but I am lonely as a skinny
old white cat with blue eyes
and irregular jagged spots of gray and black
showing a tiger pattern.
I am a tyger, I am an owl. I am some ancient wisdom
taking its own pulse and listening:
BANG!
BANG!, goes my finger.
BANG! Lover, I wish
we had bought
the purplish polish for your
toe
nails!

NEW
BRAIN

FOREMAN AND ALI
(ORANGE FLOWERS)

THERE'S A BOY BABE INSIDE OF SOME MAN
in his Past, his Present, his Future:
HE'S
IN

A

RAPT
U
R
E;

HE'S WRAPPED (FOR SOMEBODY)
around jewels he slowly concretes.
He's Forman battling Ali—all hunched
over, creating a mighty power.
—He's a furnace inside. He's alchemy
OF TENDON AND MUSCLE.
Look Mama! A huge pearl! A Porsche!
A pound of plastique to poke
IN MY EARS!
FEARS DIE IN THE BLOW UP.
HE'S DISSOLVING TIME AND SPACE
to hold her forever
in an agony she never agreed to.
He'll die with her when her death comes
—BUT
she'll swim
solo to the ocean
while he screams on the shore
showing what he forged from the fresh pork

of what HE CALLS Heart.

.   .   .   .

Meanwhile there are tall orange flowers
and fat people crashing in cars with visions
of themselves as Toltecs—
GODS

OF

CON

SUMERHOOD—
and if one pulls back the gray cloud just a trifle
there's a young dead president who smiles
AND JUST AHEAD ARE HUGE SIGNS
OF NOTHINGNESS
while a red-tail hawk soars over a house
and gravel on the roof shifts slightly
in the wind and the heat
OF

THE

SUN.
HE KNOWS IT'S ALL PERFECT;
HE KNOWS IT'S ALL PERFECT AS VELVET
AND MACHINE OIL AND CINNAMON!

WHAT MORE CAN YOU ASK OF A MAN

BUT

TO LIVE

SO

IN

TENSELY!
!   !   !

?

CZECHOSLOVAKIA

IT IS 1939 AND THE FIRST DAY OF
WORLD WAR TWO
all flapping with banners and festoons
and scrolls and tiny gray wings
and the Nazis are invading Czechoslovakia
in khaki tanks and on motorbikes
with odd-shaped grenades and mobile cannons and THIS IS
THE END OF SANITY
(coming out of the old wooden radio)
where everything is a jigsaw puzzle of red, brown
and green maps and pastiches of psyches
where truth is ripped from what is perceivable.
It is the Victory of Propaganda, roasting Asian
rice farmers
WITH NAPALM AND ARMING FREEDOM FIGHTERS
to splatter women and children
from
HELICOPTERS.
A man and his lover may find their asses
flashed to photons

BUT
A
LOVER
with a long waist
and deep eyes looking into
a mirroring mind
and making
WITH CLAY
new stones, new colored rocks
that are cartoon faces and penguins and foxes and elves
melted together
IS

THIS
REALITY
((whatever it may be))
EX
PERIENCING
itself.
THE GRAINS
of sand
are as shimmering and superb
as anything
—as wars and smooth nebulae and jazz
drifting around a candle flame
while the dishwasher groans in the kitchen,
THIS
IS
the love
that hides behind the skull and crossbones
and the splashing of gold paint
on purple silk while
children laugh
in the mortar concussions.

THE
BATTLE
IS
IN
the
EARS

&

THE STOMACH

and swirled into the eyebrows

it is thick underfoot and sticks to the shoes

stinking.

" S N O W S   O F   H O L L Y W O O D "

WHERE ARE THE SNOWS OF HOLLYWOOD?
. . . *où sont les neiges de* Hollywood?
I am the leading man among the bursting violets
I am the aficionado of glare and smog in my rayban glasses;
for breakfast I'll eat the birds' thoughts
IN THE TRUCK ROAR
while the sandy beach slides away from the ocean
and planes with big chins like Timothy Leary's
ZOOM FROM THE SMAZE.
IT'S
ALL A FLARE
and a new pair of shoes
and the blazing headlamps raise from the hood
and windows lift and fall at the touch of a finger.
—AND
THERE,
RIGHT THERE,
in the *exact midddle*
in front of Gooie Louie's
THE BLACK MAN STANDS
in his dungarees
with his hands manacled behind his back
and bent at the knees
while the navy blue cops
pat him down and he staggers
with a big grin in the heat
of the morning sun.
. . . *où sont*
Where are
les neiges
the snows
de Hollywood?
of you know where?
Where are the renegade Villon and the rocker Lennon?

Where are the old mothers weeping at their pianos?

HERE

I

AM

LOVER,

remembering your face
at the airport
and our naked bodies in the mirror.

The radio raps about perfumes
and greenblack buildings drive by on NO wheels.

MAYBE MAMA LION
for Ray Manzarek

OH
YEAH
!　　!

No,

it's *oh yeah* . . . *oh yeah* . . . ; the wound
papered over, making paper tygers
—WITH A BANDAID . . .
BANDAIDS . . . BANDAIDS . . .
—F
E
E
L
I
N
G
SO
BAD!
Out of body in the blackness.
Solid silver blackness of forty billion years
—in an agony of Crazy, knowing nothing
—looking for a self to hold the mind.
BEEN THERE MANY TIMES. BEEN THERE MANY TIMES.
The sand underfoot is just a blackness
to hold the blind. Coming back to voices:
CALI, GOING BACK TO CALI, BACK TO CALI

FORNIA,
FORNIA,

NOT TO THE
FUR
N
A
C
E
—but to the wound!

Many years covered over, still deep
S
T
I
L
L
there; TRIED TO BANDAGE IT
with long stem roses and with ferns.

((Lying on the beach watching chipmunks,
watching chipmunks and BUGS
and
ODD
patterns
ON
the leaves.
HURT IN
MY SELF ES
T
E
E
M
!

((There's a bloody war outside that's whistling
through the wound!))

stretching

out to Someone

in

a

DREAM;
IT'S NO DREAM, STRETCHING OUT TO MAMA LION
IN A DREAM.
SO BAD! FEELING SO BAD! ALL MY FRIENDS
HAVE LEFT ME
and we're eating rich food, rich food,
with the sound of silver clinking
on the finest plates
—IN CALI, GOING BACK TO CALI—
KALI,
we're eating you
in a dream. You're a salmon.
California salmon coming back to rivers
flowing from a head
on a cliff where folks look down on
the top of eagle's wings.

IT'S A GOOD LIFE!
IT'S A GOOD LIFE!
IT'S A GOOD LIFE!

(out of body out of mind)

—while the rain forests are coming down

IT'S A GOOD LIFE!

while the rain forests are coming down

Hear the crashing sound

IT'S DEEP INSIDE

Your life swinging round

your body.

Does Mama Lion love you?

Does Mama Lion love you?

DOES MAMA LION LOVE YOU?

Can the salmon drown?

BE OF GOOD HEART

for Lita Hornick

BE OF GOOD HEART! YOUR DEAR FRIEND IS AWAY,
NOT IN THE SKY, NOT ON THE EARTH.
YOUR DEAR FRIEND IS AWAY,
not in another time, but alive
and strong and will stay
in another day, in another night
and another day
where your fingers touch and your lover's
hair shines and there's moon
and sun and stars in the onliving eyes
for we all shine on
WE ALL SHINE ON
where the long cars drive through the streets
and the breeze rustles the evergreen trees
and the smell of the feast
sings from the table

—anything else is a lie and a fable.

BE OF GOOD HEART!

YOUR DEAR FRIEND IS AWAY

alive and strong

in another day, in another night
and another day
where your lips and the tips of your fingers
touch,
and there's moon
and sun and stars

in the onliving eyes

and there's moon

and sun and stars
in the onliving eyes.

BLOOM COUNTY

GRAND THEFT! MURDER! ARSON!

EATING ICECREAM! LOVING BABIES!

SLEEPING BY THE FIRE!

SCREAMING AT THE STARS!

There's a brightening sweetness on our insides
that's tangled with the ogre in OUR ARMS.
The old dear figures walking softly in the mossy dells
are meeting even older creatures in the darkest woods.
The well-groomed matron's stare inside the airport
breaks up like a rock of crack
and gospel groups are shaking through the night
inaugurating tambourines of blackmail
while big brown dogs are sleeping at our feet.
Through all of this, as minor as it seems
compared to your buttocks, I adore
the curves your nipples make upon

MY THIRSTING MIND.

.

THOUGH

SPIRIT
SHOUTS

TO
INTERWINDING

SPIRIT

IN

THE

NIGHT

TO MAKE

the world of trucks and shoes we hug in
—it is you standing on the bed with open arms
and laughing smile that is the shimmering
of my mind.

What are all the wolves and elves the Heart can find
compared with this?

In this speeding life with you
there's a redwood grove of bliss.

INDIAN

HE'S TALKING TO HIMSELF—HE'S AN INDIAN.
He's got blackbrown hair—hanging to his crack.
He's wearing a plastic leather jacket cost forty bucks.
His party nose is broken many times
up above his mustache
down below his bleary eyes
and the matching beard.
He's walking / talking to himself.
It's o.k., Brother,
ain't nothin there
can smother
passion, spirit, pride, when
you're talkin to yourself.
Down deep inside are the grizzly bears and whales
who are the brothers
that your grandpas ate—while
standing, singing in their boats
in the blueblack waves.
What language are you speakin to yourself?

We're so different.
We're so strange.
I'm a different brother.
We're mammals Brother,
speaking to ourselves.
I'm strange.
What language are you speakin to yourself?
standing in the waves
in the icy blueblack waves
singing to the brothers that your grandpas ate.
Down deep inside are the grizzly bears and whales.
Passion, spirit, pride when you're talkin to yourself
can't be smothered.

It's o.k., Brother,
I'm talking to myself.
I'm talking to myself.
Up above my mustache my party nose
is broken many times.
I'm wearing a plastic leather jacket cost forty bucks.
I'm talkin to myself I'm an injun.
I'm talking to myself I'm an Indian.

I'M AN INDIAN.

INDIAN.

SPANISH ROSES

WE COME FROM NOWHERE AND IT'S NOWHERE
WHERE WE GO.
There's not even blackness where we go;
no silver light or sparkling snow;
no smell of Spanish roses;
no night upon the town;
and when I stand up, I know I've fallen down.
I'm on a cliff top.
Don't
send
me
a frown.
Sometimes it's hard here.
The mind makes wrinkles and a frown.
You're my Lovin Darling; I'll be a man here
not some goddamn clown.
Sometimes I slip but I'm not falling down.
There's not even blackness where we go
but I'm a man here, I'm the man you know.
We come from nowhere and it's nowhere
where we go.

BRASS TACKS

for Joanne Kyger, for Gary Snyder, for Peter Coyote,
for Allen Ginsberg, for Nanao Sakaki

IT'S A BUSINESS SELLING WORDS
BRASS TACKS   STACKS
of non-stop images. Everything comes raging
through THE THROAT where the Chakra Lotus
(living spirit body) is a double Elephant
that's dancing trampling out the sounds
from seeds and shapes in the endless
MESSIAH/UNIVERSE THAT SURROUNDS
US
with White Snakes
and K-Marts
and photographs
in magazines of naked breasts
on beaches, and smells of perfume in the pages
gagging up my mind, and little yellow flowers
growing in the sand that deer might eat
if they were there standing in their naked hooves.
I GO TO WORK IN BLANK WHITE BOOKS
WITH
PENS

while my old Harley RESON-
ATES
in some space that's
NEV
ER
DEAD
and roosters crow like black pansies in the snow
leopard's roar-ing growl.
IT'S A BUSINESS WHERE
I'm lying on my late step-great-grandma's

floor on a rug before the fire
with Christmas smells around, playing
pick up sticks
with some girl I never saw
BE
FORE
and my imagination is filled with costumed DAREDEVIL
and the evil CLAW in his under-earth drilling ship
moving through the waves of stone and lead
in a zeppelin traveling through the inner world

—To my father visiting me
in his two door gray-black car
with fat wheels and a charging silver ram upon the hood
and my Aunt Maxine's sexy naked feet.
IT'S A BUSINESS SELLING WORDS
that tell that a million species are about
to die—20 percent
of all living kinds—each one as perfect
as a memory of finest dreams.
The seams of life are what we're
LETTING

F
A
L
L

A
PART

it's greed, hunger to devour, to have more people
and endless plastic, oil-burning carts
and to bring to meaty fact the looniest plans
of slick fat men plotting on the children's lives
and plotting on the lives of eagles, forests, coral reefs

It's a business selling words, brass tacks,
stacks of non-stop images to tell out loud
—it's a bigger business peddling death

IT'S A BUSINESS PEDDLING DEATH
IT'S A BUSINESS PEDDLING DEATH
IT'S A BUSINESS PEDDLING DEATH

The seams of life are
FALL
I
N
G

ALL APART
from plotting on the lives of eagles, forests, coral reefs
to make the wealth of slick fat men
at their armored stretch desks
with the engines droning soft.

IT'S A BUSINESS SELLING WORDS

BRASS
TACKS

stacks of non-stop images
to tell the seams of life
ARE FALL
I
N
G

ALL APART.

Use the shoulder of the mind to stop the ugly wheel.

Heros and heroines are always being born.

It's a business selling words!
It's a business selling words!
It's a business selling words!

—Brass Tacks!

Written for the "Eco Poetry Roundup" at the
Palace of Fine Arts, San Francisco

HE SEIZE

WHAT THE BABY BOY SEES. He sees himself full grown
in his mama's eyes. He sees the flaming
skulls and arrows and crashed planes of drugs
and death. There's no disguise / for the hate
he
sees
there.

Consciousness is a flare! And she'll douse it!

He sees

the beauteous women

with their long sleek legs

like his mama's.

The crash of a marriage.
The breasts of a daughter.

And then over the edge of the world
the mane and paws of freedom

for powerful Art
and the love of an otter

He's not a machine but a rippling man.
HE'S NOT A MACHINE BUT A RIPPLING MAN.

DOG GRACE

THE FLAMBOYANT blade is smashed through the skull.
But he stands tall.

He lifts himself because it is too far to fall

DOWN

DOWN

DOWN

> as the water flows from the tap in the sun,
> crystalline, silver, clearer than ever
> and the dog takes it in her black lips
>> loving the glory of water
>> loving the glory of water
> relishing the eternalness of this moment

> but she can't know and she doesn't care.

> And
>> it
>>> comes on in his head
>>>> like a light bulb

the meaning
the very meaning of:
> what Grace is,

ANIMAL GRACE.
No longer buried
in the mudbank of memory.

> Elegance!

DREAM WORD OPENING

HE MUST HAVE STRENGTH to touch the deep
in this existential trip.
Where the black-chinned
hummingbird perches
on the branch splattered
with pale green lichens
in the silver mist.
—Five minutes away, beggars writhe
in a damp Hell under flattened
cardboard boxes;
and we are each
very proud
of the costume
of our consciousness
as it rises up on a stem
to flower.

But it is all right.

But it cannot be! when the Good
and the Strong
do not hug one another.
When no spirit may have a brother
and
the sleek old manzanita shines in the forest

SACRED SERPENT

A ROUGH SHAPE comes out of your clay
and it is you or a smiling fox and it kneels
   but it's almost a serpent
you've left there
               as your breasts are left

      on my eyes in the mirror
      as you drive away
               in silver exhaust fumes
      through the forested canyon

      to the seething white hiss of the city
      to the white hiss of the city

         let
         there
         be
      mercy, joy and pity
      for those whose work it is
       to build souls

      with no mortar, plastique or machete
      with no laurels and confetti
      but with firm hands, bright minds

               and
                  fine
                     feet.

FREE TO BE EVIL OR SWEET

BESIDES / Besides / Besides / I don't want to be an artist
if I am moronized by my art!
Let me say
what
truth
is!
The burst and ruth of it
are fit
for a lion!
This is the Human Universe and I stand kneedeep in it!
My head's pushed like a worm into the Future!
A family swirls round me like a rose
and the smell of it made me drunken
My spirit rises up though it was shrunken
and I will
be
a

strong man

with courage   (free to be Evil or Sweet

to walk through the fields of consciousness

where the Black Fire world rubs the world
of Celestial Bliss.

ACID MEMENTO ONE

remembering the sixties

LIFT NOT the painted veil which those who live
                    call Life,
says Shelley, but I have been
                    where the psychedelics sing
making madrigals with the lumpen bodies
                    of monsters
growing into the landscape.
The colors of angels, in the real patterns
                    of Doctor Strange,
slip through the filter

    of

consciousness.

(All of this was done for consciousness.)

Never has so much been stirred
by so few molecules.

So I lay back watching
the packs of giant white wolves
and cathedrals flying through the minds
of eagles.
I knew intensely and secretly
the waves that were crashing the shores
of the coal bin in the mind's basement,

as dark eyes closed in an ecstasy of timelessness.

ACID MEMENTO TWO

remembering the sixties

WITH FREEWHEELIN FRANK in the bright sun
   —on the overstuffed couch
       we pass, back and forth,
the red-gold powder
      in the tiny toy pirate chest

Taking only a flitter of pigment on the tongue
     the room expands in a slow warm
blast
     of Hells Angel posters and leather
and velvet and swastikas and storms of Joan Baez

Then a few more tastes of the powder:
     BITTER
as koolaid.
     BITTER
as koolaid.

   I flash in the body of a hummingbird
through the smell of sagebrush
   on the high plateau of the Andes,
lofty
 as
Faust,
over infinite oil spills of the future
          where
           a
         million
         species
         die
      in the desert
        of greasy
           car wrecks.

BEYOND SOUL

HE'S MAN-MAKING! He's made himself a soul
but now he makes himself a man.
 This warm child beast blows up into a writhing mass
of loves and wants and takes and grabs
        and growths
        and poundings
floundering through the god damned
                        wave beaten shoal
    into the whole he's made.
There's an eagle, up above the truck, dive-bombed
            by *quarking* ravens.
    He sees and smells a spangled shield
            of April flowers:
        blue dicks
        wild onion
        hog fennel
blazing stars, buck brush, gilia and larkspur
(with buttercups
            and indian paintbrush).
On them he sees the face of beggars
            in the town
        with smashed nose, tooth-missing laugh
            and grinning frown.
He might be Rembrandt. REMBRANDT. REMBRANDT.

THE BRIGHT PLUMAGE

for Dennis and Katherine Hopper

HE HAS COME THROUGH and the bright plumage
        drops away
like the old music.
The path through the hazelwoods and the oaks
        is narrow
but the sky is huge.
He's pulled himself from the deluge.
Sight, Sound, Taste, Touch, Smell,
are an image of the Milky Way
        in a waterfall
of quicksilver and fire.
Quicksilver and fire
        in a waterfall
are an image
        of the Milky Way.
With Sight, Sound, Taste, Touch, Smell,
he's pulled himself from the deluge.
The sky is huge
        and narrow
as the path through the hazelwoods and the oaks.
The old music
        drops away.

Look, he has come through.
        He has come through!
           And where's the bright plumage?

        And he wears the bright plumage.

DARK CONTEMPLATION
for Jay Defeo

"AGNOSIA"—DARK CONTEMPLATION,
let me kneel to thee, let me kneel to thee,
for I have become as shallow as a small stream
that trickles through the rocks and the clay
where the bunch grass grows and the sun-cups
open their petals and smile with their sex at the sky.
I know less than the small fly
who lands on the red-veined stone.
Now I am ready to know, for nothing is known.
My mind is a worn sheet of virulent vanities.
Each small step forward laughs
with the cynicism of tragedy
and I sense there is something
dark of me,
and I sense there is something
dark of me,
that must now be quiet
and silently roar

AND

I

WOULD

BOW MY HEAD

TO ALL THINGS

that I have never seen before

and to this creature in the cave

who blinks and sniffs in the sun.

I hear from long ago
that I and my thoughts are one.

"TO GLEAN THE LIVINGNESS OF WORLDS"

replying to Rilke's Eighth Elegy

> "Animals see the unobstructed
> world with their whole eyes . . .
> But our eyes, turned back upon
> themselves, encircle and
> seek to snare the world,
> setting traps for freedom.
> The faces of the beasts
> show what truly IS to us."
>
> DUINO ELEGY
> NUMBER EIGHT

1

NOW I'LL MAKE THIS MINE:

WITH EVERY EYE IN POUNDING SKULLS

BEASTS SEE THE OPENING.

That's not true.

Nor are they in some calm state
for a leap to someplace beyond the senses' field.
Theirs is a less mental shape
of cortex, brainstem and starry tissue
—and I have been there

I have dreamed there—in fleshy hell
hoping

to break time's tissue down
and thereby crumple space to bring a heaven
near to me.

(Me, I'll crumple space up
as all creatures do,
DIS-
SOLVING TIME.)

There's no clearing out there.
NO GLADE.

It is
all
ILLUMINED BY

the arms and teeth that made it

and the laugh and cry.

2

MY EYES WERE NOT TURNED BACK
UPON THEMSELVES
but went reaching out through all the wolves and elves
that slept beneath my bed and in the corners of my head

TO OUTWARD SWEEP
and draw my love brute back to me.

My eyes were solid ghosts projected
where the world unfolds.

I see no separate oneness in the visages
of beasts
that is strange to me,
except that their clarity does not unfold
to whirl itself to fireworks
that blow my mind with lights

and with sights of this doe who stands beside
the street in bright headlights of my car
while her two plump, spotted fawns
blink toward my smile.

HEY YOU!

Hey deer, I'm on fire! You are more
comfortable,
at some moments, because your spirit
has fewer swirls and your conscious body

lives deeper back in time.

3

DEATH IS BESIDE THE POINT!
WE'RE ALWAYS DEAD

and

in

EVERY WAY
this flesh is every way alive. Our extinction

IS THE PROOF THAT WE ARE FLAMES

and the grass fire continues on, alighting
up the forest.
              Deer, you and I are the same stuff
—just slightly different mists of spirit.

I could almost be your lover.

You are almost mine.

We're Brother / Sister.

WHAT GLORY IS THIS UNIVERSE THAT THINKS!

I always become an animal
as you are always
BEING ONE;

it is one unfolding.

It is unfolding
one
to the other,
Sister, Brother.

4

BLACKBERRY BLOSSOMS ON THE VINE
and their fruits of pebbled black
and glinting red
reach out madly in the air

when not trimmed back

to accommodate
the garden of philosophy.

Layer after layer of thorny stalk and leafy stack
HURL THEMSELVES OUT
in sunny morning air
that vibrates with the cries
of mating hawks.

This is almost perfect imitation of the tiers
of stars creating us
from which we draw our juice
or blood

and on the fruit of which we clean our hooves
or tap our *fin de siècle* gloves.

SO MUCH FOR SAD PURE EMPTINESS!

SO MUCH FOR SAD PURE EMPTINESS!
where roses
bloom by castle walls.

5

THIS LIFE IS STAR LIFE;
         SISTER DEER AND I
SEE STARS WITH STARS.
          Brother puma
  bites his lover's neck and she sees
  multidimensioned
      shapes of light.

  What is in space for roses and for berries
    is the life
   that's whirling there
   WITHIN
  —within the organelles of cells

and the imagined time they took to crumple selves

 into a racing thing that's standing in the rains
  and still beyond the reach of brains.

   NO ONE EVER

    turned

     my

    HEAD

    back

   to face away

  from the world in which I
     die and play.

6

MY BODY IS PUT IN BOXES
and then the boxes are surrounded
by moving images of boxes
with myself inside of them, looking at the moving
picture, book and TV boxes.
These show those who approve
or disapprove
from their essential
teetering groundlessness in almost
unconnected boxes, and so forth,
on and on . . . till I might be deaf or dumb.

I MIGHT FORGET THAT I AM
a swirl of spirit
in an ebullient world!

AND THAT THERE IS JOY.

This is joy that I eat the sun-heated berry,
smell the rose, smile at the deer,
and flick my headlights off and on
to see if she will run.

There is pain if my fingers are pricked by thorns
or if I am crushed by cars or bombs
of if my flame is made to smolder
by a sopping blanket of what is numb.

IF I HAD A TRILLION SENSES
I COULD TELL YOU
why molecules are lies,

AND

WHAT

WE

TRULY

ARE
! ! !

—AND WHY WE BUILD THESE SOULS
and what is the perfume that they are!

.

If I had a thousand-trillion senses I could tell you
why molecules are lies
and
what
we
truly
ARE
! ! !

—And why we build these souls
and how
(if we may make one)
it may help to heal
the scar.

THE GARTER SNAKE IS THE SLEEKEST ANGEL
that I know, with his simple mind
that is inseparable from hunger
and an endless history,
whether in his spine or great black
gleaming eyes.
(He, like the sea beast beat by waves,
is the deep philosopher,
and not someone with shears
who carves out sculptured emptiness
among the scentless roses,
while pretending he can't smell.)

We're always there with death.
I'm made of death,
called *particles of matter,*
and that's one joy of life:
that I have beat out entropy
and am the whirlwind of a trembling strife.

I

HOLD

MY LOVER

in these arms
and she says my head is a sun
for her.
(Her breasts are universes lying on *my* arms.)

WE ARE EACH OTHER'S INSTRUMENT
to glean the livingness of worlds.

In each of us is something wild.
There are enough mild
dull eyes of domestic brutes that we have bred
from bird and beast
to make them part alive and partly dead.
A thousand generations in a cage
makes a helpless thing
—not even quaint
like bat-shaped cracks
in grandma's porcelain
or
moon shadows
thrown by basil on a garden wall.
The ecstatic hunger of the snake
is what I filter through this fox of reason
as I touch damp moss or steering wheel,
OR
LAUGH
AT
THE
SKY
which is a monster, living, baby cell

as am I,

or laugh at the sky
which is a monster living, baby cell

as are you and I.

What we stare out upon or sniff
is the whale tooth in the ivory jaw
and the sandgrain in the pearl
reflecting back the myriadness
of this intermingling swirl.

TWO HAIKUS

1)   OH ACCIDENT!
OH
PER
FECT
((CRUSHED))
snail
—LIKE
A
STAR

gone
out
!

2)   OH,

HUM
MING
BIRD
SHAD
OW
on the black
plum
!

((No summer lightning
though))

BEGINNING WITH A LINE
BY DI PRIMA

"The only war that matters is the war against the imagination!"
The only love that shatters
is the love of despondence and horror.
The only honor that shines
is the one that smashes
the
lust
for duty.

ANY
CRIME

THAT
DIMINISHES

THE
SOUL

is not credible

—such as:
the foulness of stuffing one's gut with the junk of greasy meat
and consumerist propaganda, of filling one's nose
and veins with drugs, of cutting the beaks from chickens & then
loading them with poisons and light and madness and eating
their eggs and spirits. BODY AND SPIRIT
ARE
ALL

ONE THING. IT IS JUST ONE WAR

AND THE BIG BOMB HAS ALREADY EXPLODED

THERE'S TIME TO LOOK YOUR LOVE
IN THE EYES AND SAY

                    no

             more

             shit!!!!!

In my insides I am a man or woman
I am heart and lung and meat and vein and breath
        going back through a deep
        phylogeny. I AM A DEEP OLD HISTORY MADE NEW
FOR THE FIRST TIME IN THE SMILING GUISE
of the universe that whispers with my breathed air
        and my soft toes. WHY THEN AM I HANDED
                    THIS
                    GARBAGE

             THESE LIES, that are told

                    over and over
             that grow tighter and tighter
        and prey on my health? Why am I diminished
             and portrayed as a fool?
AND TOLD TO BUY AND CONSUME TILL
        I AM ONLY A FOOL??

How come I am a tool of this explosion

a tool of tools in the midst of this
        SLOW MOTION BLOW UP!!!?

                    STAND
                    UP
                    !!!

STAND
UP
!!!

Get off your back and turn off the box
with the moving pictures.

Go for a walk in the woods or on the plains.
Speak to a cliff!

The only war that matters is the war
against the imagination.
The only honor that shines
is the one that smashes
the
LUST
for duty.
It is your duty to absorb the social propaganda
and become crazed with the need for overpopulation
and to stimulate the greed to devour what has been
out there for a billion years
and to burn petroleum in endless
and countless flames in the ceremonial vehicles
and the machines that change the climate.
It is duty to torment the innocent
and the less privileged

AND

TO

FINGER

&

TORTURE

&

TEASE

right out of their homes and lives, a million
species of brother and sister beings.

It is duty to dissolve any signs of an inner life
that is different in any way from the outer lies
of consumerist propaganda.
IT IS DUTY TO BE OF ONLY
One Dimension,
so that the inside soul is no different
from the commercial for tennis shoes.

The Finances
of
ROCK AND ROLL
sings anthems of cheap beer
straight into your ears
as you shove your green paper over the counter

to trade for burgers that are fried in the tallow
of cows grazed where there were once forests in the Amazon!

The only war that matters is the war against the imagination!!!

FOR CHARLES OLSON: who would understand this and see that it is about deep behavior and about knowing the desire to love and to murder, and about being moved by truth and beauty

TO KILL YOUR ENEMY WITH YOUR BARE HANDS
　　　to tear his heart out as did poet Nezahualcoyotl
　　　　　(then splashed blood in four directions);
　　　　　　and to see the gray iridescent flash
　　　　　　　on the wing of the butterfly
　　　　　　is to know the beginning of Reason

　　　　　　is to know the beginning of Reason

　　　　　when these both

happen at once.

One is the memory of reading.
The other is right in the eyes
and lands on a grass blade
then flutters away

　　　　as transient as a jade ear ring,
　　　　as permanent as summer lightning

　　　　　　as permanent as summer lightning
　　　　　on a field in the high mountains
　　　　that is dotted with elk sleeping by streams,
　　　　　tiny junipers, boulders, and fat cacti
　　　　　　pushing up like mushrooms
　　　　　to peep through the gravel.

IT

IS

MADDNESS
                (((!!!))

TO PURSUE REASON. For surely
at the end of the research
is
SOUL!

├────────┤

BECAUSE THE IMAGES WE HAVE OF HORROR
are so great

SO DEEP

SO SINGING

so great

SO DEEP

SO SINGING,

we make straw men,

scarecrows

and call them

"MY FEELING."

.

YET BECAUSE REASON IS AN ACT
and the sight of beauty is as deep as the site of murder,
there is the flicker
of a many-colored gray wing
shedding dust

and the scarlet splash of a blood drop!

/

FOR THE BIRTH OF A
NAMESAKE GRANDSON

—LIKE A RED-HAIRED BABY BORN
in lights in the night, in agonies
of contraction,
the pads of our fingers and arms

hold the weight of the tiny being in our senses.
Here's the breath-soft lightness of flannel,
and heat that stirs in the swaddling clothes

with fine blue flowers woven in down.

He's born with the power
of ancient demons (steaming
and flamey)
and the clarity
of Scottish honey

INTO
A
HELL OF IMAGINATION

and a heaven of bodies!

This impotent babe with the potency for soul
reflects back the shape
for stars to be in.

ALL THE SHAPES CREATED

of spirit and protein

are little more than the stars

that copy them. We are black neurons in the night

and we arrive with howlingly empty blue eyes

to nuzzle for Truth and elegance.

Hold the whirlwind.
                    This is the old dance,
the alchemy of genes
                    made new all over again!

THE ARTIST
for Bruce Conner

THE ARTIST has faces that are nude ladies and feathers.
Women pose in the visage of the whirlpool
    raising bare arms and arching bare thighs.
Tentacles of squid sway down among pinions
of African eagles from the artist's beret
and they tangle white hair.
  In the blackness of his face, spider webs and lichens
  are matted together making a waterfall that splashes
  down to the chin.
His head tilts down, staring into the vision.
The glow of his consciousness
        is an aureole.

  —A HUGE WHOLE THOUGHT in all of its myriadness
        is what he grasps for.
His black velvet beret is a dome of power
       in the haunted light of the room.

IT IS ALL OUT THERE.
EVERYTHING IS OUT THERE!
     It is superlatively clear.
It will all come together in connected fragments
  —oceanic!—floating—everywhere
      in the nineteen directions.
He sees it clearly—it is all so endless,
    so sensory.

His satin neckband is twisted and knotted
with demon emanations.
His gentle old jacket is awash
with mystic
wrinklings.

The jewel that he wears is a star cluster
carved out of coal.

Horseback rides are engraved on the gold frame,
        there are childhood memories of fields of grass
        with a mouth on each blade
telling stories
of the origins of pure matter and nothingness.
Foxes circle around it all
and they bark
in honor
of the softness of mulberries.

MAMMAL LIFE
on rereading Herbert Marcuse

"REMEMBRANCE OF THE PAST may give rise
                    to dangerous insights."
        Insights into this tyrannical
                        social dimension.
        The real mammal life
                        with its clear sensorium
            and the wisdom of the gut
                and the meat in the blackness
                that stretches back in time
                        to the stars
            through the bodies of strange
                            forefather beasts
        is the powerful NEGATIVITY,
                powerful negativity,
            THAT WE USE FOR OUR REVOLT.
    Mammal life is deep and luminous as the belly of a shark
            or the white fungi on cedar trunks
        in the cool rainforest
            AND
                it
                is
                me

        and it says:

            NO!
        YES!

            NO!
        YES!

    NO! to this damned one dimension!

TEETH OF IMMEDIACY
(BUCKEYE BUTTERFLY
AND CHAINSAW)

for Reinhard Harbaum

TEETH OF IMMEDIACY, TEETH OF THE MOMENT!
How infinite we are in this Hunger!!!!!
    Rage of crack and rage of the chainsaw
    chewing away soft wings of this moment.
    Dark dusty brown wings, with patterns
              of art nouveau, and gold circles of eyes
and bars of beige with perfect skitters
        of scarlet.
    Jagged chunks shot out like bullets,
    and the smell of redwood!
    Then the sizzle of the swooping transport,
    like fingers passing over
              ersatz velvet.

    This is the blow up!
        The explosion!
    Blow up of the biological context!!

Where will one go for the information density of protein?

DEEP IN

GIVE ME THE AGGRESSION in the souls of birds.
The black stuff.
The hard stuff.
The bright stuff with a glitter of play and rage
        bound together.
                        The small silhouette
flies swift and it drives beak first
            into the back of the hawk
            as she slips away in a rapid turn,
                        alert and alarmed.

Here on the freeway is a cloud of fumes!
Here on the freeway is a cloud of fumes!
Here on the freeway is a cloud of fumes!

Here on the freeway is a cloud of fumes!

Here on the freeway is the cloud of fumes

        that I drive through, with a sizzle of heat
    on black plastic.

The blue of the sky is as cold as an iceberg.

Those two spirits are wild and alive and DEEP IN!

Deep
in
depths
of their centers.

The sound of the tires is ugly and intimate.

HAIKU
homage to Buson

THE PINE CONE SHADOW
holds a sow bug.

Gravel in the asphalt

flares

white.

NOTES

"For Love," page 3. In this poem the colors of morning and the sounds of urban construction become a net holding memories of a caged jaguar seen in the Peruvian Amazon, tiny marmosets, and huge blossoms which bloom for one night at the bottom of the Grand Canyon. The poem ends with a flicker of Lord Byron's song, "So we'll go no more a roving."

"The Silken Stitching," page 7. "SMASH THE SYSTEM!" began as *écrasez l'infâme,* or *crush the abomination*—an exclamation by Voltaire that refers to the viciously grinding and entrenched system of pre-Revolutionary France.

"Awakening and Recalling a Summer Hike," page 8. A recollection of a hike through canyons and ridges with biologist-artist Hans Peeters and his wife Pam. Nesting eagles, coyotes, and nooks of old California nature created a landscape as vividly complex and alive as Keats' mind. These places recall Keats' idea that there may be an intellect of place.

"Dark Brown Eyes of Seals," page 13. In the thinking of body-philosopher H. Matthias Alexander, it is the habitual holding of the head and neck in a collapsed and crunching pattern that is the origin of many discomforts and disabilities. Freud said "Anatomy is destiny," and asserts that we are psychically formed in the experiences and fantasies of infancy. Sometimes one can feel the truth of both of these thoughts while walking in the luminous world.

"Stanzas from Maui," page 19. A poem presenting, as if it were a sculpture, the linguistic and neuronal moment in which one who is dying of one love is born into another. The repetitions have to do with the intensity and flesh echoings of experience. The poem is a reification of a deep experience.

    Kwannon/Kwan Yin is the Bodhisattva of Compassion.

"The Challenger Monument," page 38. Written at the request of Isamu Noguchi and now inscribed on a triangular granite slab below his *Challenger 7 Memorial* in Bay Front Park, Miami.

"White Boot," page 50. The Sterling in this poem is natural philosopher Sterling Bunnell, whose thoughts and conversations have been a stream of insights into nature for me for over thirty years.

"Disturbed by Freedom," page 51. Written in the beauty of Strybing Arboretum in Golden Gate Park, San Francisco, while thinking of the changes from abstract expressionism to humorous pathologies in the later work of Philip Guston.

"Foreman and Ali," page 55. The championship boxing bout between George Foreman and Muhammed Ali clearly showed two styles of physical power; Ali lengthened and moved almost weightlessly, striking out from his equipoise; Foreman hunched over, compressing his intestines into an alchemical furnace of power, and pounded blows out from there. Ali won, but barely.

"'Snows of Hollywood,'" page 59. Allen Ginsberg and Gregory Corso changed Francois Villon's refrain, "Where are the snows of yesteryear?" to "Where are the snows of Hollywood?" in an introduction to a poetry reading in the '50s.

"Brass Tacks," page 72. The Eco Poetry Roundup was organized by poet Nanao Sakaki to deepen consciousness and raise funds for the preservation of the unique blue coral reef at Shiraho, Ishigaki Island, Japan. The reef was endangered by the proposed construction of an airport for tourism. This poem was written for the event. "Brass Tacks" is dedicated to the other readers that evening.

"He Seize," page 76. This poem and the following eight poems are a subset to the *New Brain* section of Rebel Lions and are called *New Voice*.

"Dream Word Opening," page 78. I woke up with the opening words and wrote them down quickly. The structure and shape of the poem reminds me of certain Kerouac "blues" poems.

The "sleek old manzanita" shining in the forest is the pallid manzanita (*Arctostaphylos pallida*), a rare species of that tree which is found on the ridgeline of the Oakland hills.

"Free to Be Evil or Sweet," page 80. The German visionary Jakob Boehme believed that our world which we inhabit is the product of the Black Fire World rubbing against the World of Celestial Bliss.

"Acid Memento One," page 81. This poem opens with the first line of Shelley's great sonnet from 1818.

"Acid Memento Two," page 82. This poem is for Freewheelin Frank Reynolds, Secretary of the Hells Angels, who dictated his autobiography to me in 1968.

"The Bright Plumage," page 84. This poem is a wedding gift for Dennis and Katherine Hopper.

"Dark Contemplation," page 85. *Agnosia* is used in its sense of knowing through not knowing. Agnosia was the method of Dionysius the Areopagite and is also that of *The Cloud of Unknowing*. The poem was first read at a memorial tribute to the hermetic artist Jay Defeo, the most daring of the San Francisco painters.

"'To Glean the Livingness of Worlds',", page 87. This poem is a stepping stone towards a stance radically different from that of Rilke. Viewing caged animals and cultivated plants in gardens and stewarded forests can be a move in understanding our mammal nature, but our eyes are the same as those of warm-blooded beasts. In the large view there is little difference between our mental processes and those of our creature cousins. Let's celebrate the resemblances between ourselves and creatures so that we gain by knowing how much we are like them.

"Beginning with a Line by di Prima" page 98. Begins with a line from di Prima's "Rant" published in *Pieces of a Song.*

"For Charles Olson," page 102. Contains a reference to Nezahualcoyotl (Fasting Coyote), one of the founders of the Aztec empire and a poet of reputation in the Nahuatl language. In *The Aztecs*, Nigel Davis quotes an early historical source:

"It only remained to drag forth the tyrant Maxtla from his place of refuge in a steam bath and bring him to justice: And as Nezahualcoyotl entered the city, the leaders of Azacapotzalco, seeing that they were lost sought out their king, who went to hide in a temazcal which stood behind a garden, and which is a bath. With many insults, they dragged him before Nezahualcoyotl, saying that they brought him, in order that the Prince might do as he wished with him. They added that, had it not been for Maxtla and his forebears, who had always been inclined toward tyranny, the state would not have suffered such wars and casualties. They said this and much else to Nezahualcoyotl, who now had a great scaffold constructed in the square, on which he sentenced the culprit and killed him with his own hand; he cut out his heart and scattered his blood in the four directions. He then ordered that full honours should be paid to the body, and that it should be buried with all the solemnity pertaining to a great lord."

"The Artist," page 107. This poem is both a description of, and an invention based on, a collage of nineteenth-century engravings by Bruce Conner.

"Mammal Life," page 109. The opening line can be found in *One Dimensional Man* by Herbert Marcuse. It is a privilege to have known Marcuse and to read his works again in a later decade. "Cool rainforest" refers to the rainforest of the Olympic Peninsula, not far from the grave of Chief Seattle.

"Teeth of Immediacy," page 110. "Information density of protein" is taken from Lila Gatlin's *Information Theory and the Living System.*

"Haiku," page 112. The three great early Japanese haikuists were Basho, Issa, and Buson. Buson is the least known in English.